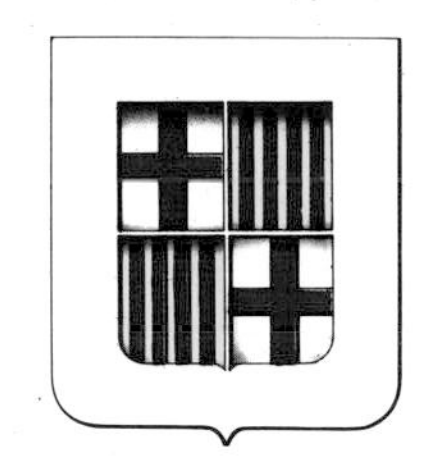

ALL BARCELONA

Text: Manuel Milián Mestre

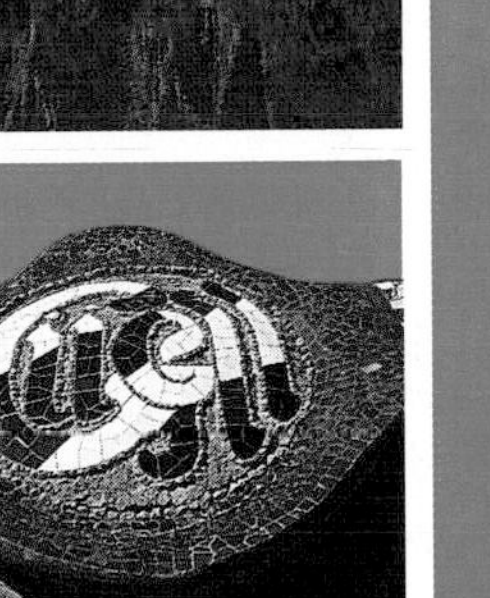

8th Edition, - I.S.B.N. 84-378-1478-2 Dep. Legal. B. 34574-1999
Printed by FISA - ESCUDO DE ORO, S.A. - Palaudarias, 26 - 08004 Barcelona

Editorial Escudo de Oro, S.A.

Museum of the History of the City: Roman bust thought to be of Antonino Pio, dating back to the 2nd century AD.

Museum of the History of the City: Roman head of the Empress Agrippina. In marble, it dates back to the 1st century AD.

BARCELONA

Perhaps the most dynamic and innovative of Mediterranean cities, Barcelona unites, on the one hand, the traditions of 2,000 years of history (the city of *Laye* was conquered in the year 133 B.C. by Lucius Cornelius Barcino) with, on the other, its characteristic propension for expansion, commerce and creativity. Few Mediterranean cities can boast of such architectural richness, such urban organisation, such culture, such transformations and such modernity as can Barcelona, many of whose exceptional present-day features were bestowed on it by the *Renaixença* in the second half of the 19th century and by the *Modernist* movement of the end of the last century and the beginning of this. The industrial bourgeoisie and the mercantile traditions held by the people of the city since the Middle Ages filled Barcelona with art and modernity, an inheritance which has made the city as it is today, one of the most fascinating in Europe. The challenge of hosting the 1992 Olympic Games has given fresh impulse to the enterprising spirit which instils the people of Barcelona, opening a new period which has seen the transformation of the city's seaboard (where the Olympic Village now stands), the mountain of Montjuïc (Olympic Ring) and the network of infrastructures and ring-roads surrounding the city.

A little history

The Roman city grew up on a small promontory, the *Mons Taber*, lying in the centre of a plain stretching between the Besós and Llobregat rivers on the banks of the Mediterranean Sea, protected from the north winds by the Collserola Mountains. The earliest plan for the city was laid down according to the classical system by Emperor Augustus between 27 and 14 B.C. Roman remains abound in the subsoil of the area which is now the Gothic Quarter, the most outstanding of which are the impressive columns of the Temple of Augustus, which rose up in the very heart of Roman *Barcino* (now in the Catalan Excursionists Centre).
The walled city continued to grow until the 4th century, when it was occupied by the Franks. Gradually, it had displaced *Tarraco* (Tarragona) as the most important city of *Hispania Citerior*, but its importance was relegated again during the Visigoth period, although King Ataulfo made it the capital of his empire for a brief period during the 5th century. The ci-

ty passed through a period of decadence with the Arab conquest of the 8th century, only beginning its recovery in the year 801 with the arrival of the French, led by Ludovic the Pious, who established a bridgehead south of the Pyrenees in what was to become the *Marca Hispanica*. It is at this time that the countship of Barcelona was born, one of the outstanding holders of the title being Wilfred the Hairy (Guifré el Pilós). Expansion and growth was a constant until the invasion of Almanzor (985), when the city was razed to the ground, forcing Count Borrell II to separate from Carolingian rule and to establish the independence of the countship in the year 988.

The period of splendour in the development of Barcelona began in the 11th century. The union of Catalonia and Aragon in the 12th made Alphonse I the first Count-King. In the 13th century, James I the Conqueror expanded his reign to the south (Kingdom of Valencia) and over the Mediterranean with the conquest of Majorca, creating the great Catalan-Aragon confederation. This was a time of rapid expansion in Mediterranean trade which also saw the realisation of the masterpieces of Gothic art and the beginnings of the great institutions (Code of *Usatges*) which go to define the historic personality of Barcelona and Catalonia as a whole.

The medieval period saw the construction of such impressive monuments as the *Consolat del Mar* and the *Llotja*, or Exchange, seat of the social institutions and guilds which wove the basic social fabric on which the bustling activity of the bourgeoisie would be based.

The Caspe Compromise (1410), granting the crown to the Castilian Trastámara dynasty, began a new period of decadence which prevailed from the 15th century throughout the Renaissance. The fact that it was in Barcelona that the Catholic Monarchs received Cristopher Columbus on his return from the discovery of America has no more significance than that of a simple anecdote.

The end of the reign of the Austrian dynasty gave way to the War of Succession, in which Barcelona sided with Archduke Karl of Austria, a misjudged alignment which caused the city to pass through another period of decline, as it was the other pretender to the throne, Philip V of Bourbon, who emerged as the victor, and on his victory Barcelona was stripped of many of its privileges. In 1714, after thirteen months of siege, the city surrendered, and harsh centralist rule was imposed on it in an attempt

Museum of the History of the City: Bronze statue (1st century AD), known as the "Venus of Barcelona".

Museum of the History of the City: Mural from the Paleo-Christian basilica (6th century AD).

preparations for the 1992 Olympic Games, which opened new horizons for the city. After 1992, Barcelona will become, inexorably, a part of a Metropolitan Community whose geographic centre will probably be Tibidabo.

Museum of the History of the City: "Diana", a fine sculpture now, unfortunately, badly damaged.

to wipe out all traces of its historical identity. Later, Philip V built the Ciutadella Castle to control the city. The short period of French occupation (1808-1813) left bitter memories. Finally, in 1860, the walls were demolished and the city began to expand into the surrounding countryside under the *Pla de Barcelona*.

The two great events around which the structure of modern Barcelona came into being are the Universal Exhibition (1888) and the International Exhibition (1929). It is between these two dates that the spirit of the *Renaixença* and of *Modernism* crystallised, with a definitive influence on the appearance of the city, comparable to the dynamism generated by

The heart of Ancient and Medieval Barcelona

Few Mediterranean cities possess such a wealth of monuments and living history. Documents exist testifying to the presence of the Iberians here, and what is now the Gothic Quarter is full of remains from the period of Roman settlement. Villas, mosaics, sculptures and so on are regularly discovered around what was the epicentre of *Barcino*, the area around Carrer Paradís, formerly the *Mons Taber*. Of its Visigoth past, dwellings and burial places have been unearthed in the Vía Laietana area, in the square occupied by the Santa Catalina market. Of the splendid medieval period there remain the magnificent architectural works, at times with more than a touch of Romanesque style, of the Chapel of Santa Llúcia (12th century) or in the Church of Sant Pau del Camp (also 12th century), formerly outside the walls.

Museum of the History of the City: Page from the Commentary on the Usatges*, painted in miniature by Jaime Marquilles in the 15th century.*

Almost all the great social institutions of Barcelona came into being within the perimeters of the ancient and medieval city, which run from the port up almost as far as Plaça Catalunya and from the Ciutadella to the foot of Montjuïc.

The Old City can be divided into three sections or quarters: the oldest, lying between the Rambles and Vía Laietana (the Gothic Quarter); the Ribera Quarter, between, on the one hand, Laietana and Comerç and, on the other, Princesa and the sea; and the Raval Quarter, which is situated between the Rambles and Ronda de San Antoni and Ronda de San Pau, once an area of convents and good works, now the haunt of the dissolute, of drug-addicts and delinquents.

The centre of the original Barcelona was where Plaça Sant Jaume now stands. The Roman forum occupied what is now the square, and this was also the meeting-place of the two main thoroughfares, the *cardo* (which continued along what are now Bisbe and Ciutat streets) and the *decumanus* (Llibreteria and Call streets). The perimeter of this early colony was oval in shape, enclosed by walls — some fragments of which have been restored — built to ward off the barbarian invaders.

In the Middle Ages, the Roman forum was the site of the construction of two Gothic palaces, seat of the governments of the city and of Catalonia (the *Generalitat*) respectively, a sign of the power of the

View of the rear, and part of the cloister of the Church of Sant Pau del Camp.

reign of the Catalonia-Aragon kingdom, with important bases on the Mediterranean.
Little remains of the Barcelona of the Visigoths except the capitals on the front of the Church of Sant Pau del Camp. However, of the late-medieval period we can still admire a number of buildings and Romanesque remains of singular, emotive beauty, such as the door connecting the cloisters with the Cathedral, probably built with materials from the Roman forum. In the Cathedral itself, there is the Chapel of Santa Llúcia, opposite the Archdeacon's Palace, which itself contains a Romanesque gallery with arches supported by 12th- and 13th-century columns.
Other remains from this era are to be found in Carrer Ataülf, near Plaça Sant Jaume, in the chapel of which was formerly the *Palau Menor*, residence of Peter the Ceremonious, who reigned from 1336 to 1397. This chapel was altered in the 16th century. One of the splendours of Romanesque is the 12th-century Marcús Chapel, on the corner of Carders and Montcada streets in the Sant Pere district. This was formerly part of the hospitaller buildings constructed by the banker Bernat Marcús and was seat of the Horse-drawn Post Guild, of great social relevance in Medieval times. Nearby stands the former Benedictine Convent of Sant Pere de les Puelles, transferred to Sarrià in 1879. This contains Romanesque capitals and the remains of the Chapel of Sant Serni, constructed by Ludovic the Pious in commemoration of the victory over the Moors in 801.
The Church of Santa Anna and surroundings — not far from Plaça Catalunya — provide yet another reminder of the Romanesque roots of the city, as it conserves its original structure, though much-altered in other ways.
The best of the Romanesque architecture in Barcelona, though, is to be found in the Raval district; here stands the tiny, delightful Benedictine

Partial view of the Roman wall.

Monastery of Sant Pau del Camp, whose existence is documented back to the year 912 and which is an exquisite jewel standing out from its depressed surroundings. New architectural projects have begun to reveal the splendour of the buildings, formed by a small church with an apse dating back to 1117 and unique in Barcelona, a 14th-century chapterhouse and a tiny, recondite cloister with double-columned trefoil arches (13th century) conferring grace and charm to the site. The entrance has an architrave supported by Visigoth capitals, proof of the antiquity of the building being further confirmed by its being the burial place of Wilfred II, believed to have been the founder of the Monastery.
The Chapel of Sant Llàtzer once formed part of a lepers' hospital between Carme and Hospital streets, currently being restored.
After this brief visit to the origins of Barcelona, the visitor can now pass on to admire its masterpieces of early-medieval art, corresponding to the period of maximum splendour of the city, the 13th to 16th centuries.

Gothic Barcelona

The architects of the years of the dictatorship of Primo de Rivera gave the name of *Barri Gótic* (Gothic Quarter) to the ancient centre of Barcelona, where an astounding pattern of Gothic buildings was built over the site of Roman *Barcino*. Use of the name was propagated by the efforts of the architect Joan Rubió i Bellver and was popularly accepted despite the resistance of some experts and historians. A visit to Gothic Barelona should start in Plaça Nova, where the Roman and medieval walls protect the magnificent Cathedral front and the rear of the Architects' College, whose functional front boasts a frieze, cheerful and Mediterranean in character, by Pablo Picasso. To the right of the towers of the wall is the Archbishop's Palace, whose Baroque front (1784) completes the square.
The Cathedral is the centre around which medieval Barcelona revolves. The original 4th-century building, certainly a church of considerable importance if we remember that a Council was held here in the year 559, was destroyed by Almanzor in 985. Its successor, a Romanesque construction, was built between 1046 and 1058. In 1289, by command of King James II, building on the present Gothic Cathdral began, completed in 1448, though the front and the magnificent dome (1913) were constructed around the end of the 19th century thanks to the munificence of the banker and mayor of the city, Manel Girona. The cathdral is crowned by two towers on the front, the dome in the centre and two splendid blunt octagonal towers, highly characteristic of Catalan Gothic.
The front is flanked by, on the left, the noble House of La Pia Almoina (16th century), where up to a hun-

Plaça de Ramón Berenguer.

Front of the Cathedral.

dred needy souls were fed daily, and, on the right, the magnificent Archdeacon's Palace, known thus as it was the residence of Archdeacon Lluís Desplà, though now it houses the Municipal Institute of History. This is a fine Gothic-Renaissance (16th century) building whose origins go back to the 11th century, with a charming inner courtyard.
Inside the Cathedral, the visitor will be moved by the austere style, the harmony of the fluted columns and the elegance of the ribbed vaults with their superb polychrome keystones. The interior consists of three aisles with ambulatory and an light-filled apse, containing jewels of art and history.
The high altar was consecrated in 1337, the magnificent choir of the central aisle dates back to 1390, whilst the equally fine marble retrochoir was added in the 16th century, blocking the view of the central aisle.
Below the high altar is the exquisite Crypt of Santa Eulalia, patron saint of the city, martyred in the 4th century, and behind it, supported by four columns, is the alabaster tomb, finely wrought by a follower of Nicola Pisano.
Of outstanding interest are: the Baptistery Chapel, with its marble founts (15th century); the Chapel of San Olegario (1405), with its wrought-iron gate darkened by praying hands and the smoke of devotional candles placed by the people of Barcelona in honour of the Christ of Lepanto (16th-century wooden sculpture), which accompanied John of

Austria at the Battle of Lepanto. Presiding the altar, at the feet of the majestic crucifix, is the tomb of Bishop Olegario. The side and ambulatory chapels contain many altarpieces, mostly from the 14th and 15th centuries: that of the Visitation (15th century) in the Chapel of San Miquel; that of the Transfiguration, a masterpiece by Bernat Martorell, in the Chapel of El Patrocini; that of the Archangel Gabriel (14th century) in the Chapel of Santo Cristo: those of Saint Martin and Saint Ambrose; that of Saint Clare and Saint Catalina (mid-15th century); and many more. To the right of the altar are the sarcophagi of Ramon Berenguer I and his wife, Almodis, founders of the Cathedral. In the Chapel of the Holy Innocents is the Gothic tomb of Bishop Ramon d'Escales.
To the left of the transept is the doorway of Sant Ivo, leading to the outside. This contains the oldest elements of the original Romanesque building. To the right of the high altar is the sacristy, containing the Cathedral treasure, a collection of objects of great

Porta de la Pietat (Gate of Pity).

Gate of San Ivo.

The crypt of Barcelona cathedral.

artistic and material value, such as the great processional monstrance, mounted on the throne of King Martin I, a silver monstrance dating back to 1390 and the 15th-century reliquary, adorned with the Golden Fleece of Charles V who, in 1519, convoked the knights of this illustrious order in the Cathedral, attended by Archduke Maximilian of Austria, and whose coats of arms and emblems can be admired in the monstrances of the choir.

The cloister, with its fine Gothic arches, is reached either through the Flamboyant Door of Santa Eulalia (16th century), through the Door of Pity in the street of the same name (Carrer Pietat) or from the interior of the Cathedral through the Door of San Severo on the right of the transept, or through the entrance to the Chapel of Santa Llúcia. Beside the Romanesque door of San Severo is the niche containing a washbasin, the double body of the fount crowned by a representation of Saint George. Opposite is the Chapel of Santa Llúcia, consecrated in 1268 and one of the few elements preserved from the old Romanesque cathedral.

The 15th-century chapterhouse contains a large proportion of the heritage making up the Cathedral Museum: remains of medieval altarpieces or panels painted by such great Catalan artists of the Gothic period as Jaume Serra (*San Onofre*, 14th century) or Jaume Huguet (altarpiece of San Bernardino, 15th century), or other outstanding contemporaries, Bartolomé Bermejo (*Pietà*, 15th century) or Sano de Pietro (*Virgin and Child*, 15th century). Also exhibited are sacred objects, such as miniature painted missals (that of Santa Eulalia, by Ramon Destorrent) or codices.

Close by is the Archbishop's Palace, with its elegant courtyard, in a mixture of styles typical of buildings constantly being added to. In a quiet backstreet nearby is a tiny square of remarkable harmony which gives its name to the Baroque oratorium, *San Felipe Neri*, constructed in 1752 and of austere exterior. It contains an aisle and a dome over the transept. The Baroque altar is frequently the setting for concerts of holy music or chamber pieces which blend in harmoniously with the contemplative silence of this tiny square flanked by two noble buildings, the seat of the Shoemakers' Guild, now the Footwear Museum, and that of the Boilermakers' Guild.

A little further on, we come to the magnificent Baroque Church of San Severo, built between 1698 and 1705, and in Carrer Bisbe, the Canons' House, communicated with the Palace of the *Generalitat* by a Neo-Gothic bridge, charmingly romantic, constructed by Joan Rubió in 1926. The Canons' House, of irregular groundplan, dates back to the 14th century, though much altered since then. It is now the official residence of the President of the *Generalitat*

View of the central nave of the cathedral.

The famous Christ of Lepanto.

(autonomous government of Catalonia). This street, the heart of Gothic Barcelona, leads into Plaça Sant Jaume, civic, political and historic centre of the city since earliest times. Its origins go back to an extension made to the Roman forum, and from medieval times until the 19th century it was the site of the Church and Cemetery of Sant Jaume. The square as it appears today was begun in 1823 and was completed with the opening of Jaume I and Ferran streets, which also lead into the square, and with the building of the new front of the Town Hall, perpendicular to the old front giving onto Carrer Ciutat.
The principal building in this square is the Palace of the *Generalitat,* seat of the institution of autonomous government which has its origins in the *Corts Catalanes* (Catalan Courts), brought into being in the 12th century by Peter the Great, and in which were represented the Church, the aristocracy, the army and the cities. The Gothic lateral front overlooking Carrer Bisbe is the oldest of the four, constructed in 1416 by Marc Safont, author of the exquisite Chapel of Sant Jordi (1436).
The interior courtyard, reached by passing under a low arch, is a true delight of Catalan Gothic. In 1425, Safont built the most beautiful staircase leading to a Gothic gallery, in front of which is the Flamboyant front of the Chapel of Sant Jordi, to whom is dedicated the entire building and whose image is to be found in numerous places here. To the left is the famous Courtyard of the Orange Trees, in the centre of which a splendid fountain serves as a pedestal for another statue of Saint George. The courtyard contains two busts, one of Enric Prat de la Riba, the other of Francesc Macià, responsible for the restoration of the Generalitat and its most illustrious president during the II Republic, by Subirachs (1983).
The Courtyard of the Orange Trees is surrounded by various chambers, such as the Council Chamber, or Golden Chamber, richly decorated with murals and crafted panels. Another is the recently-restored Torres García Chamber (1914), named after the Uruguayan author of the murals to be seen here, hidden for decades. Nevertheless, the most majestic of the rooms is that of Sant Jordi, with three aisles and vaults and a cupola supported by huge pillars, a 16th-century masterpiece by Pere Blai, decorated with frescoes, and yet another statue of Saint George, by Frederic Marès.
The Renaissance-style main front, overlooking the Plaça Sant Jaume, is also the work of Pere Blai, projected in 1597 and completed in the 17th century. In the central balcony over the main entrance is a sculpture by Andreu Aleu (1867) and another fine version of Saint George, this time on horseback killing the dragon with his spear.
The other important monumental building in this square is the Town Hall, the origins of which govern-

A spectacular view of the fountain in the cathedral cloisters.

Chapel of Santa Llúcia.

The archdeacon's house. Partial view of the ground floor with a fountain in the middle.

mental organ go back to the 13th-century *Consell de Cent* (Council of One Hundred), formed by leading citizens and representatives of the guilds, artisans and tradesmen and, from the 16th century, the army. These Catalan institutions, in existence since the 14th century, were abolished in 1714 by Philip V. The present Town Hall was built over the house of Simó Oller, acquired in 1372 in order to build the seat of the *Consell de Cent*, later the *Saló de Cent*, central body of the palace as it is now, a work designed by Pere Llobet (14th century). Between 1399 and 1402, Arnau Bargués added a new section in Carrer Ciutat, its 14th-century Gothic front conserved to this day. After the Church of Sant Jaume was demolished in 1823, the building was extended to its present dimensions and was completed in 1847 with the addition of a Neo-Classical front overlooking the square, the work of Josep Mas.

Shortly after this, in 1860, the Sessions Chamber was constructed, also known as the Queen Regent Chamber, as it is presided over by a portrait of Queen Maria Cristina with her son, Alphonse XIII. This is where the city council meets. The superb *Saló de Cent* was also extended at this time, and this amply-proportioned chamber is reserved for the most solemn occasions. In 1926, Josep Maria Sert decorated the *Saló de Croniques* with representations of the Catalan expeditions to the Eastern

Mediterranean during the Middle Ages.

Of the interior, outstanding are: the vestibule, reached through a doorway in the front flanked by sculptures of King James I and Councillor Joan Fiveller, defender of the liberties of the city in the 15th century; the black marble staircase (1926) which leads to the main floor; the Mayor's Office, decorated with paintings by Xavier Nogués and featuring frescoes on the ceiling by the Modernist artist Ramón Pey; and the chapel, with works by the sculptor Monjo. The vestibule and main floor are a veritable museum, containing works by Llimona, Clarà, Viladomat, Gargallo, Rebull, Marès, Miró, Hugué, Navarro and Subirachs.

Finally, the administrative buildings were completed in 1969 with the opening of the new building in Plaça Sant Miquel, its front adorned with motifs by the sculptor Subirachs.

The other side of the Cathedral district has as its central point the Plaça del Rei, one of the most harmonious, evocative sites in the city. Due to large-scale restoration work in the 1920s, in which ex-

Courtyard of the Archbishop's Palace.

An overall view of the Plaça del Rei.

Close-up of the monument to Ramon Berenguer. ▷

cavations took place in Via Laietana, many of the treasures contained in this sector of the Gothic Quarter are now revealed to the gaze: the restored Eastern section of the wall, with abundance of Roman remains at its foot, reaching a height here of up to nine metres, with three 18-metre high towers; the Chapel of Santa Agueda with its octagonal belltower; a large section of the Royal Palace; the elegant spires of the Cathedral; and the pleasant cypress garden beside the wall, in which stands the equestrian statue of Count Ramón Berenguer III, the work of J. Llimona.

Equally splendid is the view from within Plaça del Rei, an impressive Gothic panorama dominated by the tower of the 16th-century *Mirador del Rei* with its five series of semicircular arches, which looks down on the dependecies of the *Palau Reial Major*, residence of the Catalan-Aragon monarchs. To the right is the beautiful 14th-century Chapel of Santa Agata, composed of a single Gothic aisle with main arches supporting a polychrome wood coffered ceiling. The high altar contains a masterpiece of Catalan art by Jaume Huguet (1464) featuring themes from the Adoration of the Magi and the Crucifixion, known as the Condestable Retablo. At the end, under a large arch, is the semicircular stairway leading to the Royal Palace. To the left is the *Palau del Lloctinent*, whose construction was approved by the *Corts* in 1457 but which was not completed until a century later. This fine palace is a jewel of Late Gothic, with many

The interior of the Chapel of Santa Agueda with, in the background, the Condestable retablo.

Plaça de Sant Jaume and the Palau de la Generalitat.

Renaissance elements in the exterior and clearly Italian influences in its interior design. It now houses the Archives of the Crown of Aragon, with more than four million documents, in some cases going back as far as the 9th century, from the Royal Chancellory, the Bailiwick of Barcelona and the Royal Audience. However, the most beautiful section of this building is undoubtedly the interior of the Royal Palace, with the majestic Tinell Room, constructed in the reign of Peter the Ceremonious between 1359 and 1362 by Guillem Carbonell. The Catholic Monarchs are believed to have received Cristopher Columbus here on his return from the discovery of the New World in 1493. Close to this square is the Gothic-style *Casa Clariana-Padellàs*, home of the Museum of the History of the City, transferred here from Carrer Mercaders. This interesting museum contains important collections of archaeological and historic remains, unearthed during various excavations, as well as pottery, coins, plans, models, paintings and documents illustrating the history of the city of Barcelona.

The Marès Museum, housed in an annex of the Royal Palace, contains important collections of Gothic and Romanesque sculpture.

But Gothic Barcelona is by no means limited to just this Cathedral district. Carrer Hèrcules leads to Plaça Sant Just, where stands the ancient Church of Sants Just i Pastor, documentary evidence of whose ex-

Palau de la Generalitat: Gothic Gallery and Golden Room.

istence goes back to the 9th century, but whose present design is of the 14th and 15th centuries. Its front is crowned by a single belltower, a second which had been planned originally being left incomplete. The interior, with just one aisle, contains interesting altarpieces, such as that of Saint Felix, a 16th-century work by John of Brussels and Pedro Núñez. One of the prerogatives of this church, granted in 1282, is that of the Sacramental Testament, under which the intestate moribund could make their will orally before witnesses who, present and under oath, were legally empowered to execute the last will and testament of the deceased.

This site also contains the 18th-century Moixó Palace, property of the counts of Sant Mori, with splendid etchings and a fine inner courtyard, the oldest fountain in the city, that of Councillor Joan Fiveller (1367), restored in the 18th century, and the singular beauty of the 13th-century palace of the Countess of Palamós, now the seat of the Academy of Letters, situated at the end of Carrer Bisbe Caçador. On the other side of Via Laietana is the grandiose Church of Santa Maria del Mar, masterpiece of Catalan Gothic architecture, outstanding jewel of the city in its splendour, grace and elegance. The district in which the church stands was formerly known as Vilanova de la Mar, and was the dwelling-place of sea-farers, merchants and craftsmen. To this day there is still here a medieval flavour and appearance to these streets. Carrer Montcada, with its old rambling houses and fine palaces, was

Palau de la Generalitat: Courtyard of the Orange Trees.

Carrer del Bisbe.

Front of the Town Hall, view of Carrer Ferran, and a Modernist shop.

at one time the most noble street in the city. The district grew up between the 11th and 18th centuries and the Church of Santa Maria del Mar was the crowning piece of this period of vigorous expansion. The original church is mentioned in documents dating back to the 10th century, though the present building was commenced in 1329.

The exterior has a rather rigid aspect, with a main front characteristic of Catalan Gothic, splay doorway and gable, tympanum with a statue of the Virgin and an enormous Flamboyant mid-15th-century rose window which replaced the original, destroyed in 1428. Two characteristic octagonal towers flank this front, which is adorned with large Gothic windows containing 15th-century stained glass pictures, as are the sides. Outstanding of these are those of the Final Judgement over the left-hand aisle, that of the Ascension of the Virgin in one of the side chapels and that of the Coronation of the Virgin in the front. The interior is an astounding architectural masterpiece, a splendidly free and open space, thanks to the peculiarity of the octagonal pillars, unusually graceful. The presbitery is a prodigy of stony height, with elegant ribbing and an air of lofty grandeur.

Not far from Santa Maria del Mar, facing the sea, is that other exceptional monument to Gothic civil art, the Exchange or *Llotja*. The original portico, sheltering traders and merchandise, was transformed in the 14th century, under the reign of Peter the Ceremonious, into this fine building with its Neo-Classic fronts. Work began in 1380 and was com-

Town Hall. Interior of the Saló de Cent *and Gothic side front.*

Front of the Church of Santa Maria del Mar.

Church of Santa Maria del Mar: a view of the interior.

pleted in 1392. The magnificent Gothic chamber, with three aisles and six semicircular arches covered in polychromed wood, was the pattern for many other similar works of civil architecture constructed in the Kingdom of Aragon.

The Neo-Classical front is the work of Joan Soler, restructured in 1771. The superb marble stairway has an Italian air, as does the upper gallery.

Many of the names of the streets and squares of this quarter make reference to the trades plied in them during medieval times: *Vidrieria* (glazing), *Esparteria* (esparto work), *Argenteria* (silverwork), *Olles* (pans), *Peixateria* (fishmongering) and so on. Along Malcuinat we come to the *Fossar de les Moreres*, formerly the cemetery of Santa Maria del Mar, rebuilt in 1989 and where tradition holds that the patriots who died defending the city in September 1714 are buried.

Exploration of the nooks and crannies of this medieval quarter will reveal reminders of its venerable past at almost every step: Gothic fountains with hanging gardens (1402) in the square in front of Santa Maria del Mar; ancient arcades; (*carasses*), grotesque stone masks placed over entrances or under balconies. However, it is in Carrer Montcada, between Princesa and the Born, where the flavour of these ancient days is best captured. In Carrer Flassaders there still stands the old coin factory, *La Seca*, which functioned until the year 1836.

Montcada was urbanised by Guillem Ramon de Montcada in the 12th and 13th centuries in order to link the districts of Sant Pere de les Puelles and Vilanova de la Mar. Its noble magnificence is illustrated in the Cervelló-Giudice Palace (16th century), now the Maeght Gallery, the 17th-century Dalmases Palace — since 1962 the seat of Omnium Cultural — with one of the most beautiful courtyards in the area, and the Berenguer d'Aguilar Palace (15th

Courtyard of the Picasso Museum.

Picasso: Harlequin - © by S.P.A.D.E.M. Paris, 1970.

Picasso: Paloma - © by S.P.A.D.E.M. Paris, 1970.

Picasso: One of his numerous versions and interpretations of Las Meninas by Velázquez. © by Cercle d'Art. Paris 1970.

LA
CHATA
P.R.R.
AÑO D 1899-

Courtyard of the Dalmases House.

Picasso: La Margot - by S.P.A.D.E.M. Paris, 1970.

Picasso: La Chata - by S.P.A.D.E.M. Paris, 1970.

century) and the palaces of the Baron of Castellet and of La Meca, both 18th-century constructions, these last three now housing the Picasso Museum, inaugurated in 1963. Also interesting are the Palace of the Marquis of Llió (16th century), now the Textile Museum, and the Gothic Nadal Palace (15th-16th centuries).

Other interesting aspects of the Gothic Quarter are the *Call*, the medieval Jewish quarter, and the section near to the Rambla. These streets are full of shops, antique sellers, restoration workshops, art galleries and secondhand bookshops, particularly Petritxol — opened in 1465 — Portaferrissa, Nous Banys, La Palla or the streets around Plaça del Pi, the scene of markets selling antiques and herbal products.

A final visit should be made to the Gothic Church of Santa Maria del Pi, whose origins go back to the 10th century, though work on the present building began in 1322 and it was consecrated in 1453. There is a 16th-century crypt and its austere front contains a huge, beautifully-perforated rose window. The

View of the Tinell Room.

13th-century side door is also interesting. The interior consists of a single wide aisle flanked by side chapels. The octagonal belltower, 54 metres in height, is one of the symbols of this popular district of traders and craftsmen. Nearby, in the street of the same name, is the Church of Santa Anna, originally a Romanesque building but containing a large number of Gothic elements of great beauty, such as the 15th-century cloister.

The Raval district contains one of the most outstanding examples of Gothic civil architecture to be seen in Catalonia, the *Hospital de la Santa Creu* (Hospital of the Holy Cross), a superb work constructed on the initiative first of Guillem Colom and later under the patronage of Pau Ferran. The hospital goes back originally to the 10th century. The main work was completed in 1415, new elements were finished in 1509 and the entire building was reconstructed in 1638.

Also worthy of a visit are: the inner courtyard and hall (1655-1678) of the *Casa de la Convalecencia*, with two galleries of fine arching and a statue of Saint Paul (Lluís Bonifaç, 1677); the former Surgeons' College, now seat of the Royal Medical Academy, with its extraordinary central courtyard dominated by a 17th-century cross mounted on a fine Solomonic column of white and pink marble. This fine Gothic construction now houses the Library of Catalonia, the Institute of Catalan Studies and the Massana School of Applied Arts.

Also in the heart of the Raval district is the Centre de Cultura Contemporània de Barcelona and the new Museu d'Art Contemporani de Barcelona (MACBA). The building, designed by Richard Meier, stands in Plaza dels Àngels. Its construction began in 1990 and was completed in the spring of 1995. The labyrinthine character of the area is in stark contrast with the complex architecture of the MACBA, with forms ranging from flat elements and rectilinear windows to curved and undulating spaces in consonance with the contemporary spirit of the museum collection.

The opening of the MACBA signifies recognition and representation of the different artistic currents which have emerged during the second half of the 20th century, making a visit to the museum obligatory for an understanding of the artistic and cultural scene in Barcelona.

The MACBA, or Barcelona Museum of Contemporary Art.

Carrer de Petritxol, and exhibition of paintings in the Plaça del Rei.

Gothic Barcelona is completed by the Monastery of Pedralbes, of which we will speak later on in this book.

Barcelona opens up to the sea

The *Rambla* is the soul of the city, ''the most beautiful street in the world'', in the words of Somerset Maugham. This avenue begins in the nerve-centre of the city, Plaça Catalunya, where all the main arteries of the city meet, the resting place, amidst large flower beds, of pigeons and pensioners. Two large fountains adorn this wide space, along with a statue by Josep Clarà (*The Goddess*), the bronze *Allegory of the City* and *The Shepherd* by Pablo Gargallo. Under the square, too, there is a bustling network of shops, car parks, two metro lines and the railway lines with their respective stations. From this point, following the *Rambla,* we reach the Gate of Peace (Portal de la Pau), dominated by the statue of Columbus perched on his high column. Years ago, a stream ran through this area, close to the second walled perimeter of the city.
The *Rambla* has different names, beginning with the stretch known as Canaletes where the waters of a bronze fountain, it is said, speed the return of all visitors who drink them.
The next stretch is the Rambla dels Estudis, thus named after a university, closed and transferred to Cervera by Philip V and now occupied by caged birds and other pets on sale. Here is the Church of Nostra Senyora de Betlem, the work of Josep Juli around the year 1680, the Tabacos de Filipinas building and the 18th-century Moja Palace, an interesting building containing paintings by Vigatà and J. Flaugier.
Here begins perhaps the most picturesque stretch of the *Rambla,* populated by newspaper kiosks open 24 hours a day and by florists, who give this section its

Marés Museum. Partial view of one of the rooms.

name, *Rambla de les Flors*, though its original name was Rambla de Sant Josep. On the right we see the Palace of the Vicereine, constructed in 1775 by the Viceroy of Peru, Manuel Amat, who did not live to enjoy his creation, though his widow made her residence here. The *Pla de la Boqueria* will be of great interest to gourmets, for it is without doubt the market with the most exquisite foodstuffs in Barcelona, as well as being the most beautiful and the liveliest, containing Modernist elements within its metallic structure.

Pla de l'Os, with mosaic by Joan Miró, marks the threshold to the next stretch of the Rambla, the *Rambla dels Caputxins*, where we find the city's famous opera house, the *Liceu*. Construction began on 11 April 1845 on the site of the Convent of Discalced Trinitarians, and the opera house was opened on 4 April 1847. This temple for Catalan music-lovers has had more than its share of troubles: firstly, the building had to be completely rehabilitated after a fire on 9 April 1861; next, an anarchist, Santiago Salvador, threw two bombs into the audience. Only one exploded, but over twenty people were killed nevertheless. Finally, another fire on 31 January 1994 destroyed the *Liceu* almost completely, only the façade looking onto the Rambla being saved. Thus was lost

The Rambla.

one of the works which best represented the splendour of the Catalan bourgeoisie of the time, with its fine baroque interior with marble vestibules, elegant staircases and typical salons of the period. Immediately this latest tragedy was announced, events began to be organised by the institutions and civil society alike, to raise funds for the reconstruction of this beloved opera house. Extended to one side, the new *Liceu* now has greater seating capacity and improved infrastructure.
All the great artists of the last century and a half have performed here, and some achieved fame in this very opera house, such as Victoria de los Angeles, Montserrat Caballé or Josep Carreras. Its repertory is vast, though the strains of Wagner have been a leitmotif throughout its history. The opera and ballet seasons here are the finest in Spain.

Various views of the Rambla. 

We are now on the frontiers of *Chinatown*, which in places invades the Rambles themselves. You can smell the sea in the streets of Sant Pau, Unió, Nou de la Rambla, in the last of which is the Güell Palace (1888), of singular decoration and architecture, characteristic of the work of its author, Antoni Gaudí. This palace is now the Museum of Dramatic Art.
At this point we can make a visit to Plaça Reial, on the left-hand side of the Rambles going down towards the port. An integral part of Romantic

The Canaletes Fountain.

MERCAT
SANT JOSEP
LA BOQUERIA

PELETERIA
NAPA

VALDÉS

burda
burda
neue mode
LAVANGUARDIA
LAVANGUARDIA
LAVANGUARDIA

JOYERIA

Front, and stalls, of the Liceu Opera House.

Barcelona, it is composed in a style between Napoleonic and Colonial in an exotic setting where tall palm trees compete with the roofs of houses of equal height on all four sides. This is a rational, picturesque square, with lamps by Gaudí and a fountain in the centre crowned by the Three Graces (19th century). It was urbanised after the destruction of the Convent of the Capuchins in 1714 at the hands of the soldiers of Philip V, and the subsequent disentailment in 1835. Its designer was Francesc Daniel Molina, who was commissioned for the project in 1848. The visitor can relax with a glass of beer under the porticoes of the square, which on Sunday mornings is converted into the bustling haunt of collectors perusing the stamps and coins displayed in the specialised market held here.

Lower down, the Rambla broadens out towards the sea, and the docks of the port come into sight in the background.

The Rambla de Santa Mónica contains, amongst its restaurants, sex shops and bars, several notable buildings, such as the March Palace (1776), seat of the *Conselleria* for Culture. Also here is the Wax Museum, housed in what was formerly a bank. This contains a collection of more than 300 wax figures

Gran Teatre del Liceu: the great concert hall, the house lights on, as it was before the fire in 1994.

Interior of the Palau Güell.

representing a huge variety of politicians, showbusiness personalities, scientists and fictional characters.
The Rambles end at Portal de la Pau, amongst mid-19-century buildings, the now restored Parish Church of Santa Mónica, and the ultra-modern Santa Mónica Art Centre, an admirable rehabilitation of the 17th-century convent. It is at this point that another of the historic facets of the personality of Barcelona comes into view; its quality of Mediterranean city. The sea stretches out before us under the gaze of Cristopher Columbus, standing on his cast iron column more than 50 metres in height. This statue, which has become one of the most distinctive symbols of the city, was conceived in 1886 by the architect Gaietà Buigas i Monravà. Inside the column, a lift takes visitors up to the foot of the 8-metre high sculpture of the admiral and explorer, the work of Rafael Atché.
Facing Columbus in Portal de la Pau, backing onto the Rambles, are the Royal Boatyards, the former Cannon Foundry and the seat of the military government. To the sides of the statue are the Customs Building (1896-1902), guarded by winged sphinxes, and the historic building of the Junta for Works in the Port, at the foot of which is the embarkation point for the beloved «golondrinas» – pleasure boats – of the city, which take visitors to the breakwater of the old port. However, to get a better view of the port, the visitor is recommended to take a ride on the cable car which runs at a height of 107 metres from the towers of San Sebastián and Jaume I to Miramar on Montjuïc.
The metamorphosis will not affect one of the most interesting medieval sites in the city, the Drassanes or Royal Boatyards, whose origins go back to the times of James I the Conqueror (13th century). The imperative need to expand out over the Mediterranean led Peter II to extend the original boatyard, a task which was completed in the 14th century by Peter III the Ceremonious. And so were born these medieval boatyards of splendid integrity and beauty,

Plaça Reial.

then the finest in Europe, designed by Arnau Ferrer and with capacity to build up to 30 ships simultaneously. Here were built the galleys which took part in the conquest of Tunisia and in the Battle of Lepanto (1575). An interesting visit may be made to the Maritime Museum, housed here since 1941 and occupying three huge 14th-century aisles. Its exhibits include figure-heads, navegational instruments, historically important caravels and galleys and an atlas dated 1493.
A walk through this area towards the Breakwater (Rompeolas) reveals a whole world in decline, that of seafarers and fishermen. Of it, all that remains is the *Barceloneta district*, one with an air all its own. The *barrio* stands on a stretch of land reclaimed from the sea since the 17th century when the quay of the modern port was built. It is now a labyrinth of streets where the people of Barcelona come to eat seafood and fish in one of its many restaurants.
One of the great achievements of the city of Barcelona, spurred on by the 1992 Olympics, was the recovery of its sea front. The Port of Barcelona, now divided into the old and the new, the Port Vell and the Port Nou respectively, has been regenerated as part of the latest initiatives. A modern pedestrian «catwalk», known as the Rambla de Mar, leads to Maremagnum, a shopping, leisure and gastronomic centre situated in a privileged position over the Mediterranean Sea. With an area of 39,000 square metres,

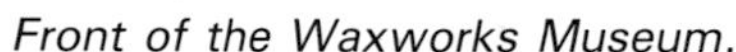

Front of the Waxworks Museum.

Aerial view of the Rambla.

Maremagnum is the latest thing in shopping and leisure, with bars, terraces, boutiques, restaurants and even a minigolf and an eight-screen cinema. The Port Vell also contains the Aquarium, the largest in Europe and the most important in the world on the theme of the Mediterranean. In it, an 80-metre glass-walled tunnel runs through an immense circular oceanarium containing 4,000 specimens, whilst 21 fishtanks bring the visitor closer to the world of sharks, goldfish and a further 8,000 animals and plants from over 300 different species. Next to the Aquarium is Imax, the only cinema in the world combining three large-format projection systems.
The Barceloneta district is reached from the Pla de Palau, where the Sailing School is located. This emblematic district also contains the Museu d'Història de Catalunya, housed in the Palau de Mar. This is also the starting-point of Avinguda de la Nova Icària, gateway to the Vila Olímpica (Olympic Village), a new district including the Port Olímpic, where we find the two tallest buildings in Barcelona: the Hotel Arts and the Torre Mapfre, as well as many bars, restaurants and terraces, open all year round.
The *Passeig Marítim* (Sea Front) forms a balcony over looking the, planned at the beginning of this century, though not actually built until 1954 and now extended to link up with the *Passeig Nacional.* The origins of the Barceloneta district are military, thanks

The monument to Columbus.

View of the Port Vell. Monument to Columbus and Maremagnum.

to the project drawn up by the military engineers Pedro Martín Cermeño and Francisco de Paredes. Work on it began in 1753 under the command of Captain General the Marquis of la Mina. The plan was a symmetrical one of octagonal streets and long blocks composed of square sites on which houses of equal height, groundplan façade could be built. Though subsequently the original plans were somewhat altered, the basic features are retained, with fine squares, such as that containing the Church of Sant Miquel, a Baroque church constructed between 1753 and 1755 to Jesuit-Roman canons by the architect Damià Ribas. Alterations to the Barcelona seaboard nowadays allow a much better view of Passeig de Colom, where there is the building of the Capitanía General, occupying the former Convent of Mercedarians, behind which can be admired the top of the *Basilica of la Mercè,* constructed between 1765 and 1775 by Josep Mas, partly of Gothic remains from the former Church of Sant Miquel and conserving a 15th-century Renaissance-style side door. The church contains a 14th-century Gothic statue of Our Lady of Mercy, patron saint of the city, the work of Pere Moragues. The people of Barcelona hold Nostra Senyora de la Mercè in profound reverence and dedicate the annual festivities of September to her. Nearby is the *Plaça del Duc de Medinaceli,* urbanised in the 19th century. This square contains the monu-

Royal boatyards and monument commemorating the Battle of Lepanto.

ment to the Admiral Galcerán Marquet by Daniel Molina. Next to the Plaça del Palau are the well-known porticoes of the Portxos de Xifré, under which is to be found one of the oldest and most popular restaurants in Barcelona, Les Set Portes, founded in 1838 and with one of the richest culinary and literary traditions of the Belle Epoque. Opposite is the splendid neoclassical front of the Llotja.
The Pla del Palau, flanked by the Civil Government building and the interesting metallic construction of the railway station, becomes the Avenue of the Marqués de Argentera as the tree-lined paths of the Ciutadella Park come into view, the last stop on this itinerary.

Interior of the Maritime Museum.

Maritime Museum: the galleon of John of Austria.

The Olympic Harbour.

Bogatell Beach.

The Hotel Arts and the Torre Mapfre.

The main post office.

Nostra Senyora de la Mercè. 14th-century polychrome statue.

Church of la Mercè.

Overall view of the Port Vell and the Palau de Mar. In the Background, the Mapfre Tower and the Hotel Arts.

Panoramic view of the quay known as the Moll de la Fusta. «Cara de Barcelona» and the «Gambrinus» restaurant, designed by Javier Mariscal.

«Francia» railway station.

The waterfall in the Ciutadella Park.

The Ciutadella Park

This magnificent park evokes memories not so sweet. On the fall of Barcelona into the hands of Philip V (first Bourbon monarch and responsible for the abolishment of the liberties of the Catalans) in 1714, the Duke of Berwick ordered the construction of a military citadel to stand guard over the city. To this end, much of the Ribera district was demolished, work on the Ciutadella beginning in 1715 to plans drawn up the Flemish architect Verboom. As a fortress, its existence lasted little more than a century, as the *Junta de Vigilancia* began demolition work in 1841, though work was halted and restoration ordered by General Espartero two years later, much to the disgust of the people of the city. Finally, thanks to the good offices of the Catalan General Prim, on 12 December 1869 the citadel was granted to the city for its conversion into a park. This new function admirably suited the organisation of the Universal Exhibition of 1888, whose seven pavilions were constructed in the park and surrounding area. The architects of the present excellent layout of the park were Josep Fontserè and Elies Rogent, and of its military past only the Governor's Palace, the chapel and the Arsenal remain.

Statue of the «Dama del Paraguas».

Mamooth.

This haven of peace within the city, with its flower beds, lily ponds, waterfalls, fountains, lakes, bandstands, monuments, palm trees and pleasant shady tree-lined paths, also contains many interesting buildings with widely differing functions. The gardens are the work of the Frenchman Forestier, and the centre of one of the ponds is adorned by one of Josep Llimona's most characteristic sculptures, *Desconsol* (Distress), which, together with the Romantic statue of the Lady of the Umbrella, by the sculptor Roig Solé, have become veritable symbols of the city. The park contains an impressive collection of works by 19th- and even 20th-century Catalan sculptors: Fuxà (statue of Buenaventura Aribau), Clarà (monument to the Catalan volunteers of the First World War), Llimona, and so on. There are also the busts of such illustrious Catalans as Milà i Fontanals, Maragall, Batlle, Aguiló, Teixidor, Fontova, Vilanova, etc. The spectacular monumental waterfall was designed by Fontserè with the cooperation of that genius of Modernism, Antoni Gaudí, then a mere student. This fountain is completed by the *Quadriga of the Aurora* by Rossend Nobas and is decorated with sculptures by Venanci Vallmitjana.

Of the buildings contained in the park, of outstanding interest are: the red-brick *Castle of the Three Dragons*, now the Zoological Museum, a work projected by Domènech i Montaner in 1888, now recognised as a pioneer Modernist building; the *Hivernacle*, constructed with iron and glass, the design of Josep Amargós, now the scene of cultural events; and the *Umbracle*, a brick and wood construction (Fontserè). The former Arsenal, now the Palace of the Catalan Parliament, deserves special attention, for this is a remarkable building which housed the collections of the museums of Fine Arts and of Archaeology between 1900 and 1932, when it was adopted as the seat of the Catalan Parliament, a state of affairs which lasted until 1939. In 1945, it became the Museum of Modern Art, which is still housed here

A nook in the Ciutadella Park.

despite the revival of its political function with the recovery of democracy and the restoration of the Catalan Parliament in 1980.
The Museum of Modern Art possesses several important collections, from Neo-Classical works by Flaugier, Lacoma, Vicente López, etc, to the Catalan artists formed in Rome in the 19th century, Pelegrí Claver, Lorenzale, Benet Mercadé, Rigalt, and the realists of the same period, Martí Alsina, Arcadi Mas, Pellicer. The museum contains excellent works by the best Catalan painters of the last two centuries, with particular emphasis on Marià Fortuny, whose two classic pieces, *The Vicarage* and *The Battle of Tetuan* are exhibited here, as well as works by: Joaquim Vayreda and the landscape painters of the Olot school; the exceptional portraits of Ramon Casas; the superb gardens painted by Santiago Rusiñol; the gypsies of Isidre Nonell; and works by Joaquim Sunyer, Canals, Urgell, Anglada Camarasa, Mir, etc. Catalan art of the last two hundred years is excellently represented, and not only in terms of painting, for the sculptors of Catalonia also make a distinguished contribution to the museum, which holds works by Manolo Hugué, Llimona, Clarà, Casanovas, etc.
Barcelona Zoo is another attraction for visitors to the Ciutadella. The Zoo is a peaceful place with an enormous variety of species of animals and an aquarium where dolphins perform. The chief attraction is,

Various species to be seen at Barcelona Zoo.

The Modern Art Museum.

"Paris Landscape", by Ramón Casas.

"The Vicarage" (fragment) by Mariano Fortuny.

''The Castle of the Three Dragons'', now the Zoological Museum, the work of the architect Domènech i Montaner.

however, the albino gorilla, a rare animal born in Spanish Guinea (now Equatorial Guinea), popularly known as *Snowflake* (Floquet de Neu).
This itinerary ends at the *Arc de Triomf*, in its day the entrance to the 1888 Exhibition and which commands a fine view of Passeig de Sant Joan. The Arch, whose architect was Josep Vilaseca, is in red brick with stone decorative elements, with a certain air of *Mudéjar* architecture. At the top is a beautiful frieze by Josep Llimona, with winged angels on the false columns seeming to direct the visitor's steps towards the new district of the *Eixample*, where the astounding aesthetic style universally recognised as belonging to Barcelona — Modernism — awaits to be discovered.

Modernist Barcelona

The Eixample (''extension'') district has in terms of town planning come to characterise Barcelona.
It was born of the need for space, as in the 19th century population density had reached frankly insalubrious proportions. In 1854 the government of Espartero and O'Donnell convinced Queen Isabel II that the walls of the city should be demolished by royal decree so that the Cerdà Plan could be carried out. The vast cultivated plain surrounding the city offered the conditions for the execution of a remarkable concept in town planning and the imagination and vision of its creator, Ildefons Cerdà, provided the inspiration for such an ambitious project. In the words

of Lluís Permanyer, "The Eixample possesses two singular qualities which make it unique in the world: it is a pioneer work of modern town planning, and it contains the greatest concentration of plastic art in the world". Catalan nationalism provided the remaining ingredients.

The Eixample begins at Plaça Catalunya and covers a vast area of the modern-day heart of the city. Cerdà's idea was to construct a garden-city, composed according to a grid plan of intersecting streets, with the inner spaces between the blocks of dwellings dedicated as peaceful leisure areas for their inhabitants. This last aspect suffered important changes at the hands of speculation and private ambition.

On leaving Plaça Catalunya and the Rambla, we see that the architectural style of the new city bears absolutely no resemblance to that of the old city. Plaça Catalunya covers an immense area of more than 50,000 square metres and is the starting point of,

The Arc de Triomf, in Passeig de Sant Joan.

Two views of Plaça Catalunya.

amongst other important byways, Ronda de Sant Pere and Ronda de l'Universitat which, together with Gran Via, form the sides of another square, Plaça de l'Universitat, where the *Literary University* was constructed in the 19th century by the architect Elies Rogent. The University building is rectangular in shape with belltowers at each end and two quadrangular courtyards with double galleries in the interior. The assembly hall is decorated in the Mudéjar style revived in the 19th century.

Carrer Balmes, which follows the line of the underground train of the Sarrià line, perpendicularly from the sea to the mountain, commands good views of the city. Parallel to this street runs the Rambla de

Catalunya which, together with Passeig de Gràcia, forms the essential nucleus of the Eixample. This shady, lime-lined Rambla is the ideal meeting-place thanks to its terraces, its cafés, cinemas and art galleries. At the intersection with Diagonal is the Serra House, now the seat of the *Diputació*, the work of the architect Puig i Cadafalch. A short way from the Rambla, in Carrer Aragó, is a building constructed by Domènech i Montaner in 1880 which now houses the Tàpies Foundation of Contemporary Art. The building has been magnificently restored and the en-

The University, and a view of Passeig de Gràcia.

The front of the Tàpies Foundation.

Aerial view of the Serra House, now the seat of the Diputació.

tire front has been crowned by a surprising metallic structure.

However, the principal artery of this section of the Eixample is Passeig de Gràcia, a wide boulevard lined with plane trees, built along the path which formerly linked Barcelona with the village of Gràcia, from which it takes its name. Beginning in 1890, the Catalan bourgeoisie built their finest houses here, composing the most splendid and colourful Modernist section of the city. At numbers 2-4 are the Sagnier Houses (1890) and at numbers 6-14 the Rocamora Houses (1918), the creation of the Bassegoda brothers. Several of the 19th century palaces, such as the Marianao Palace, have now disappeared, but on one corner stands the Lleó

Morera House, designed by Domènech i Montaner, with its floral ornamentation.
The architectural eclecticism of Modernism is demonstrated in the so-called *Block of Discord*, to be found in this same section of Passeig de Gràcia, on the left. This is a series of buildings, unique in themselves, in which the differing concepts of their authors seem to do battle. At number 43 is the spectacular Batlló House by Gaudí, at number 41 the beautiful and harmonious Amatller House by Puig i Cadafalch and at numbers 39 and 37 are two Sagnier houses, standing next to that of Lleó Morera.

Further along, at number 82, we are confronted by a paroxysm of Modernist architecture, that masterpiece by Antoni Gaudí which is the Milà House, popularly known as *La Pedrera* (the quarry). This building caused furore at the time of its completion due to its accumulation of avant-garde elements and daring touches. Many believe this house to represent the zenith of Modernism and to be one of the most singular 20th-century buildings in the world. This is an enormous stone monument full of undulating forms with an air shaft of extraordinary distorted shapes, as if the very stones were fluid, organic. The

The Amatller (left) and Batlló (right) houses.

The Lleó Morera House.

Two views of the Casa Milà, known popularly as "La Pedrera" (The Quarry).

chimneys and ventilation points on the roof become phantasmagorical warriors, abstract mosaic spirals, a fantastic forest of prodigious imagination. The profound astonishment awakened by the architecture of the Milà House diminishes somewhat as we admire the remaining buildings lining the Passeig de Gràcia: the Robert Palace on the corner of Diagonal; the house at number 96 by Rovira i Rabassa which belonged to the painter Ramón Casas, near to the restaurant *La Punyalada*, patronised by Modernist artists and their followers; number 112, one of the Sagnier houses; number 113, by Falqués; and the Fuster House, built in 1912 by Domènech i Montaner.

Along Diagonal, at the intersection with Passeig de

A view of the Diagonal, and a partial view of the Eixample district.

Plaça de Francesc Macià and Avinguda Diagonal.

Plaça de Sants and Parc de l'Espanya Industrial.

A spectacular panoramic view of modern Barcelona.

Sant Joan, there is the monument to the poet Verdaguer, in the form of a gloriette.
There are two bullrings in Barcelona: *Las Arenas*, in Plaça d'Espanya, near to *Escorxador* (Slaughterhouse) Park, containing gardens and a characteristic sculpture by Joan Miró; and the *Monumental*, on Gran Via de les Corts Catalanes, with a Moorish, Mudéjar air.
But we can close this chapter with mention of two more masterpieces of the Modernist art of Barcelona, the *Palau de la Música Catalana* and the *Hospital de la Santa Creu i Sant Pau*.
The *Palau de la Música* was designed in 1908 by Domènech i Montaner to be more a cathedral of music than a mere concert hall, as it was to be the home of the *Orfeó Català*, the choral society founded by the maestro Lluís Millet, architect of the renovation and re-evaluation of Catalan music. The *Palau* is considered by some the crowning point of the Modernist style, after which most of its features are fashioned, though it also contains a good many elements of *Art Nouveau*. It stands near to Via Laietana, between the districts of San Pere and Santa Catalina.
The *Hospital de Sant Pau* is another outstanding work produced in this extraordinary period of the artistic history of Barcelona. The different sections of the hospital are located in separate pavilions surrounded by gardens and linked by paths in an atmosphere of peace and tranquility fostered by the artistry of the beginning of this century. The hospital is reached along Avinguda Gaudí, a majestic backdrop to the gates and bevelled main front. The architect of the project was Lluís Domènech i Montaner (1902). The front, crowned by an elegant tower, is a characteristic element of Modernist architecture.

''Woman and Bird'', by Miró.

Palau de la Música: concert hall.

Overall view of the Hospital of Sant Pau.

Torre Figueres, also known as "Bellesguard".

The entrance to the Güell Pavilions.

The Barcelona of Gaudí

This is a Barcelona clearly differentiated from the Modernist, for Antoni Gaudí left his mark on the city so strongly as to transform it. In the words of Joan Bassegoda Nonell, a leading expert, "Gaudí experienced to the full the euphoria of the *Renaixença* and Modernism, but was a part of neither, for his peculiar vision of life and architecture kept him aloof from politics and the artistic movements in fashion".
A Gaudí itinerary through Barcelona, coming down from the mountain to the sea, would begin at the Figueres Tower, also known as *Bellesguard* due to its location at number 16 of the street of the same name on the site of a royal residence dating back to 1408 over whose ruins Gaudí built this mansion between 1900 and 1909, its elements clearly reminiscent of Gothic architecture. Its fine tower is crowned by a four-armed cross. In Avinguda de Pedralbes, not far from the monastery, are the Güell Pavilions, the stables and lodge of what was once the Güell family estate, now the gardens and dependencies of the Royal Palace.
The Teresian College (C/ Ganduxer, 85-105) is a singularly austere manifestation of the artistic vision of Gaudí, designed at the request of his friend and

founder of the Order, Enrique de Ossó, between 1888 and 1889.

Above Plaça Lesseps, Park Güell (C/ Olot) is one of the marvels of Gaudí which, nevertheless, was never terminated. It has been a public park since 1923, owned by the city, as the original idea of Eusebi Güell to create a garden city on the *Muntanya Pelada,* following the English model, did not finally prosper. The steps at the entrance to the park immediately stir the imagination as we are greeted by a dragon centrally placed on the way to the large space known as the Salon of the Hundred Columns — though in reality there are but 84 — which was to house the market-place of the projected community. The columns, Doric in form, support tiny spherical cupolas on which the upper square stands, offering one of the most beautiful views of the city. This park, declared Patrimony of Mankind by UNESCO in 1984, is one of the most exceptional illustrations of the genius of Gaudí and his vision of architecture integrated with its natural surroundings.

At Carrer de les Carolines numbers 18-24 is the *Casa*

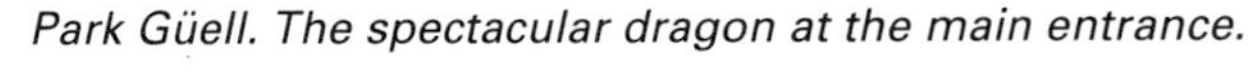

Park Güell. The spectacular dragon at the main entrance.

A detail of the sculpture of a central element of the main staircase.

Two views of the Güell Park.

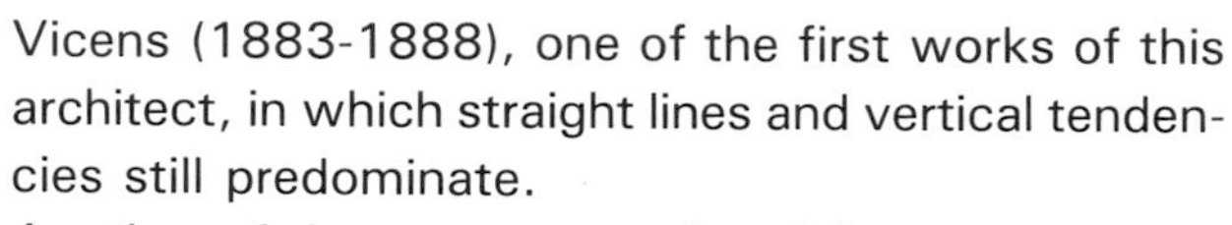

Vicens (1883-1888), one of the first works of this architect, in which straight lines and vertical tendencies still predominate.

Another of the greatest works of Gaudí, described in the preceding chapter, is the *Casa Milà* in Passeig de Gràcia, also declared Patrimony of Mankind in 1984 by UNESCO.

The *Casa Batlló* (Passeig de Gràcia, 43), totally remodelled between 1904 and 1906 by Gaudí is, as we mentioned above, a masterpiece of undulating artistry, of the rounded forms of the mature period of the architect, its interior a delight to the senses.

Casa Calvet (C/ Casp, 48) was built between 1898 and 1900, its ground floor containing offices and furniture designed by Gaudí himself.

The southernmost point of this route is marked by the Güell Palace (C/ Nou de la Rambla), close to the Rambla. Built between 1886 and 1888, this is defined by Bassegoda Nonell as "Gaudí's first great work of architecture, in which his personal vision of architecture is made manifest".

But a tour of the works of Gaudí in Barcelona can only terminate in one place, the Church of the Sagrada Familia. Here, we are confronted by the vision of the genius, by his mystical dream of redemption as he suddenly rediscovers forgiveness and grace for a people which wishes to expiate its sins or render worship to the Creator. Gaudí, inspired by the medieval idea of religion, dedicated his whole life to this project, bequeathing a colossal challenge to posterity which has still not been acquitted and which has been the cause of much controversy. The architect inherited the idea of a Neo-Gothic church, its crypt already at an advanced stage of completion, from Villar and Martorell, the latter involving the young Gaudí, who was just 31 when he put his visionary genius to the task of designing an awesome cathedral 110 metres in length and 45 high, with three fronts each bearing four soaring towers (a total

Aerial view of the Sagrada Familia.

Night-time view of the Front of the Birth. ▷

of 12, dedicated to the Apostles), four monumental belltowers (one for each Evangelist) and two colossal domes, dedicated to the Virgin and to Christ respectively, the latter reaching a height of 170 metres. This ''20th-century cathedral'', as it is known, has a Gothic basilical groundplan in the shape of a Latin cross, with five naves connecting with a transept from which stem another three naves, apse and ambulatory. The architect's awesome vision pursued a staggering sense of verticality, a meeting-point between the earth and the sky, between God and Humanity. The original idea of Antoni Gaudí for this tremendous undertaking included a universe of Christian symbols, of theological ideas and biographical references to Christ, an aspect which can be clearly seen in the fronts which, according to the plans, will be three, dedicated to the Birth, the Passion and the Death and the Resurrection.

Work came to a halt in 1936 due to the outbreak of the Civil War, and Gaudí's study, containing his plans and drawings, as well as the crypt, were destroyed by fire. A start was made again in 1952, thanks to the persistence of his disciples and followers, using drawings and models saved from the fire, and in 1954 work began on the front of the Passion (west), with its four towers. This was completed in 1976 and decorated in 1987 by the sculptor Josep M. Subirachs.

Sagrada Familia: Front of the Passion.

Entrance to Montjuïc Castle.

Montjuïc: from the International Exhibition of 1929 to the Olympic Games of 1992

Barcelona is contained by the sea and the mountains. Next to the port rises the mountain of Montjuïc (173 metres), dominating the fascinating view over crowded city bustling at its feet, and at the other end of the city is the Collserola Sierra, dominated by Mount Tibidabo, another huge natural space offering the delights of peace and relaxation and which will form one of the splendours of the Barcelona of the future: 7,000 hectares of forest parkland in the heart of the city. Montjuïc, inhabited in the third century B.C. by the Iberians, is today one of the largest, most lovely of the parks of Europe, crowned by a castle dating back to 1640, extended and fortified in 1694. Since 1960, this has been the Military Museum of the city.

The 20th century opened with magnificent prospects for this mountain and will close with its development complete, the entire mountain transformed into a huge cultural, sports and leisure area which will be renowned throughout the world. Firstly, the Universal Exhibition of 1888 saw the urbanisation of the slopes of Montjuïc looking over the city. Next, in 1929, the northern half of the mountain was occupied by constructions designed to house the International Exhibition. This development is best view-

The interior and exterior of the Palau Sant Jordi.

ed from Plaça d'Espanya, at which point converge the main arteries of the Gran Via, Carrer Tarragona and Paral·lel.

Paral·lel was in the 1920s the centre of the *dolce vita* of the city, the haunt of Bohemia, and it was in Plaça d'Espanya that the Exhibition of 1929 was born. On one side of this square stands Las Arenas bullring, on the other two brick towers imitating the belltower of Saint Mark's in Venice, flanking the Avinguda Maria Cristina and affording a breathtaking perspective of the architectural complexities of the Palau Nacional, the backdrop to a light-filled spectacle at dusk when the extraordinary fountains designed by Carlos Buigas are illuminated, a sight by themselves making this a worthy visit. In the centre of Plaça d'Espanya is the creation of Jujol, a disciple of Gaudí: a huge fountain adorned by the sculptures of Oslé symbolising the three seas of the Iberian Peninsula, the Mediterranean, the Atlantic and the Cantabrian.

Of the exhibition buildings lining Avinguda Maria Cristina, interesting are the palaces of Communications and of Metallurgy on the left and those of the Quinquagenary and of the Nations on the right. The wide square containing the monumental illuminated fountains also house the palaces of Alfonso XIII and of Victoria Eugenia (the work of Puig i Cadafalch). The water of the fountains, thanks to the talent and technical skills of Buigas, compose melodic variations and spectacular configurations of splendid colour and evanescence. Dating back to the same period is the pavilion designed by Mies van der Rohe and which represented Germany in the 1929 Exhibition, a landmark in the history of architecture, with its simplicity of geometric forms and materials; marble, onyx, glass, water, chromium-plating and so on, and for its distribution of space.

The immense form of the Palau Nacional, with its

Aerial view of the Olympic Stadium.

Various views of the illuminated fountain, Montjuïc.

Palau Nacional.

four belltowers and its central dome, covers a surface of 31,000 square metres and consists of two storeys. This palace contains a majestic ball-room holding 20,000 people, once the scene of splendid social occasions, and now houses the Museum of Catalan Art, currently undergoing extensive reorganisation at the hands of the Italian architect Gae Aulenti. The museum will be of tremendous interest to all lovers of art. Created by Lluís Pellicer, his successor Folch i Torres further enriched it with the transfer here of the great murals of the finest Romanesque art in the world, previously conserved in tiny medieval churches of the Catalan Pyrenees: apses such as that of the Church of Sant Joan de Boí, or the renowned Church of Sant Climent in Taüll, with its exceptional 12-century Pantocrator; impressive Virgins and Apostles of deep, burning colour, whose relationship with Byzantine art is immediately apparent.

This extraordinary museum contains an important collection of medieval Catalan pictorial art, Gothic and Romanesque, with invaluable carvings and bas-reliefs, altarpieces and statues, where are represented the greatest names of this period of Flemish influence, Lluís Dalmau, Jaume Huguet and other 15th-century masters. But there are also collections of masterpieces from the 16th, 17th and 18th centuries, with splendid pieces representing the work of Pedro Beruguete, Juan de Juanes, Morales, Velazquez, Ribera, El Greco and Zurbarán, as well as fine ceramic works from the 14th to the 18th centuries.

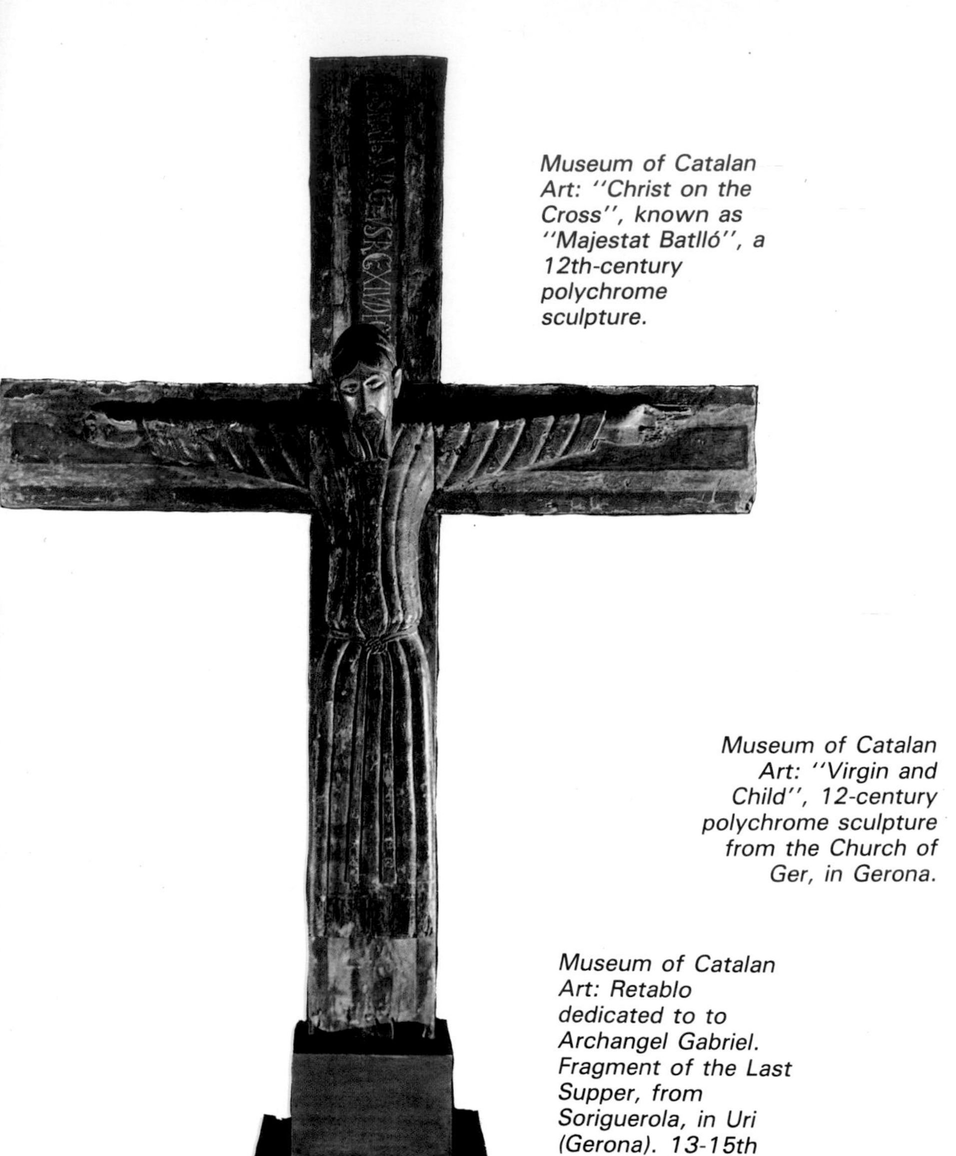

Museum of Catalan Art: "Christ on the Cross", known as "Majestat Batlló", a 12th-century polychrome sculpture.

Museum of Catalan Art: "Virgin and Child", 12-century polychrome sculpture from the Church of Ger, in Gerona.

Museum of Catalan Art: Retablo dedicated to to Archangel Gabriel. Fragment of the Last Supper, from Soriguerola, in Uri (Gerona). 13-15th centuries.

Museum of Catalan Art: Pantocrator. Fragment of the mural decoration of the main apse of the Church of Sant Climent, in Taüll (Lerida). Considered the most valuable 12-century piece.

Museum of Catalan Art: ''La Verge del Consellers'', by Lluís Dalmau (1445).

But this mountain reserves more than one surprise for the visitor, such as the string of museums, including the Archaeological and the Ethnological museums, or the theatres, such as the *Mercat de les Flors*, and classical amphitheatres, the Greek Theatre, where summer festivals are held, or the splendid gardens with their fountains and shaded paths, or the Albéniz Palace, the residence of illustrious guests, with rooms decorated by Salvador Dalí. Farther on among the tree-lined, snaking walks, the visitor will delight to the most avant-garde design to be seen in Barcelona: the Miró Foundation, housed

in an ultra-modern building of architectural splendour, the work of J. Lluís Sert (1974).
Montjuïc holds pleasure not only for adults but also for children: a funfair, which can be reached by cable car from Paral·lel, with a vast array of amusements; sights such as Miramar or the castle which perches at the top of the mountain, offering a breathtaking panoramic view of the city and its port; and innumerable shady spots where pleasurable rest may be taken after a long walk. But perhaps the greatest charm of Montjuïc for the tourist is the Spanish Village (Poble Espanyol): a walled area whose entrance is through the towers and gateways of Avila, where in 1929 the beauty of popular architecture from the whole of Spain was recreated. This picturesque anthology was conceived and constructed by Xavier Nogués, Miquel Utrillo and Ramon Raventós after study of the medieval, Renaissance and Baroque architecture of the regions of Spain. This work was directed by the architect Francisco Folguera, commissioned by Barcelona City Council.
With all this, the crowning, definitive touches were put to Montjuïc in 1992, when the city of Barcelona hosted the Olympic Games, and the mountain became the main venue for the sports competitions. Preparations for this great event entailed the com-

Museum of Catalan Art: Polychrome sculpture depicting the "Maiestas Domini" (12th century).

Panoramic view of the Miró Foundation.

plete reorganisation of infrastructure on the mountain, with the creation of new spaces and improvements to accesses. The principal works were grouped into the so-called Olympic Ring - *Anella Olímpica* - on the south side of Montjuïc, where praiseworthy efforts were made to harmonise modern architecture with the historic surroundings. A good example of this is the Olympic Stadium, the magnificent setting for the main athletics events and the Olympic Games opening and closing ceremonies. The original front, dating to 1929, was maintained and rehabilitated, adapting it to the new project by architects V. Gregotti, F. Correa, A. Milà, J. Margarit and C. Buxadé.

On the esplanade adjoining the stadium is the Sant Jordi Sports Centre. This remarkable and unusual building was designed by the Japanese architect Arata Isozaki, and is covered by a 45-metre high metallic spatial network. Nowadays, the Sant Jordi Sports Centre is the venue for a variety of important sports and cultural events. Nearby are the Bernat Picornell Swimming Pools, the venue for the swimming events at the 1992 Olympic Games and also an excellent viewpoint over the entire city. The rest of the south side of the mountain was landscaped and developed to form an enormous, 52-hectare park.

But Barcelona, asphyxiated by lack of space, has

Monument to the Sardana.

Spanish Village. Gate of Avila.

opened up new ground beyond the mountain of Tibidabo. This new expansion has made necessary the building of ring-roads and of the Vallvidrera Tunnel, crossing the mountainous mass of the Collserola Sierra, destined to become the epicentre of the great Barcelona of the future. This mountain range, just five kilometres from Plaça Catalunya, will be the site of the world's largest urban park, 7,000 hectares of forest park and 500 hectares designated for leisure activities and facilities. A park 20 times larger than Montjuïc, eleven times the extension of the Bois de Boulogne in Paris and 22 times the size of Central Park in New York. With six million trees and just a few developed zones, Collserola will be the great green belt of the Barcelona of the 21st century.

For the tourist, there can be no better way to bid farewell to this city than by ascending Tibidabo. The most practical route by car is to take the Arrabassada, or Avinguda del Tibidabo at the end of Carrer Balmes, where the Tramvia Blau, the only tramline remaining in the city, a relic of its history, takes travellers to the *Peu del Funicular* — the foot of the cable car. Nearby is the Science Museum, one of the most interesting and popular of Barcelona, sponsored by the Foundation "La Caixa".

The funicular railway takes us up to the top of Tibidabo, at an altitude of over 500 metres and now bristling with telecommunications antennae and the great Telecommunications Tower, designed by the architect Norman Foster, with a total height of 288 m. Situated on El Turó de la Vilana, 445 metres above sea level, the Torre de Collserola, as it is known, has a public viewpoint offering splendid panoramic views over the city, its metropolitan area and up to 70 kilometres into the distance.

A modern, up-to-date funfair – originally created by Dr. Andreu – is a delight for adults and children alike, and the facilities here range from an Automat Museum to excellent restaurants.

The «Tramvia Blau», which began service in 1901.

Casa Arnes.

Collserola Tower.

The Church of the Sagrat Cor, designed by Sagnier, obeys the same expiatory idea as does the Sacre Coeur in Montmartre, Paris. The site was personally chosen by Saint John Bosco when he visited Barcelona during the last century. A great statue of the Sacred Heart crowns the dome of this neo-Gothic edifice.
From Tibidabo, with its hazy contemplation of the horizon over the sea, the city clustered at its feet and the green of the forests behind it, the not only sees the city of Barcelona in all its extension, but also commands an unsurpassable perspective of the history of the city. In its woods, excursions can be made to the Fabra Observatory, or to Vil.la Joana, with its tiny museum dedicated to the foremost of Catalan poets, Verdaguer, or to Vallvidrera, Les Planes, La Floresta or Valldoreix, lying between the woodlands and the new motorway connecting Barcelona with the Vallés rural district.
To the right of this scene, Barcelona seems to want to flee along its great Diagonal, where in the Pedralbes district is a taste of the Barcelona of the future, with huge, functional buildings, such as the

Aerial view of Tibidabo, with the city in the background.

seats of the Banca Catalana and of La Caixa, and profoundly innovative constructions, such as the Trade buildings, designed by the architect Coderech, luxurious hotels — Princesa Sofia, the Hilton — and the university campus, which stretches across the entire access to the city, from the Cervantes Park to the stadium of a unique institution which transcends the purely sporting; *Camp Nou*, home of Barcelona Football Club — *Barça* — with a multitude of 100,000 members and grandiose installations built in the 1960s as one of the largest stadiums in the world, a venue at which huge crowds of passionate fans support a team which, as the local saying goes, is "more than a club".

The final stop-off on this tour will be Pedralbes, a residential area which has grown up around the Gothic monastery founded in 1326 by Elisenda de Montcada, fourth and last wife of Jaume II, the most paradisal location in Barcelona, with a three-storeyed cloister adorned by Gothic arches supported by slim pillars and elegant capitals. The building was completed in 1419. The exterior features a lovely octagonal belltower, unfinished, and an austere Gothic front with splay doorway and the coats of arms of the Montcada dynasty. Inside, the church contains a single, majestic aisle, 14th-century stained glass windows and the tomb of its founder, Queen Elisenda, with alabaster statue. The 15th-century chapterhouse, or Chapel of San Miquel, with frescoes by Ferrer Bassa (1343) depicting scenes from the life of the Virgin, gives marvellous testimony to the beauty of Catalan Gothic art, which within this

Camp Nou, the home of Barcelona Football Club.

walled monastery reached one of its maximum points of expression.

More worldly, resting among bushes and trees, with pools and pretty paths, the *Palau Reial*, residence of Alphonse XIII, though in fact little used by this king, was built between 1919 and 1929, taking its inspiration from the country palaces of Renaissance Italy. A visit to this palace reveals richly decorated rooms, such as the Throne Room, with carpets and royal tapestries, magnificent porcelain and furniture, clocks, fans and paintings. An interesting Carriage Museum will provide the visitor with a glimpse of our ancestors' means of transport.

Barcelona, city of culture

One of the outstanding features of the people of Barcelona is their love of culture and of collecting. Since the Middle Ages, Barcelona has been blessed with numerous collectors, and thanks to these were born private institutions, foundations and museums, yet another demonstration of the creativity of the inhabitants of this great city.

If curiosity was felt by all for the various themes — art, costume, sculpture, painting, historic objects, flora, fauna, archaeology, ethnology, pottery, music, the sciences, machinery and so on — the depth of this vocation was due in large degree to the culture spread by the universities, the oldest of which still conserves its 19th-century Arts building and Rectory, with courtyards and gardens, in the square which bears its name – Plaça de l'Universitat. This is now known as the University of Barcelona, more popularly the Central University, and its campus has now been transferred to the Pedralbes district, which offered more space for the new faculties created in the 1960s and 1970s. To this were later added the Autonomous University, with campus in Bellaterra (Vallès Occidental district), the Polytechnic, its departments scattered all over the city and environs, and the more recently-founded Pompeu Fabra and Ramon Llull universities. Over 50 museums await culture-loving visitors, not to mention many more private collections of similarly high standing, such of those set up by different industrial families and which will, without doubt, in the future increase the cultural heritage which can be admired in Barcelona. This was the way the Frederic Marès and Textile and Costume museums or, more recently, the Antoni Tàpies Foundation (C/ Aragó, 255), the Thyssen-Bornemisza Collection in the Monastery of Pedralbes, and the Barbier-Mueller Museum of Pre-Columbian Art Foundation (C/ Montcada, 14), were created.

Monastery of Pedralbes.

PALAU SANT JORDI
PISCINES BERNAT PICORNELL
ESTADI OLÍMPIC
PG. OLÍMPIC
AVDA. DE L'ESTADI
NOU JARDÍ BOTÀNIC
PARC DEL MIGDIA
PASSEIG DEL MIGDIA
CAN VALERO
MUSEU MILITAR CASTELL DE MONTJUÏC
JARDINS MOSSEN JACINT VERDAGUER
TELEFÈRIC
PL. MIRADOR
PARC ATRACCIONS MONTJUÏC
FUNICULAR MONTJUÏC
JARDINS MOSSEN COSTA I LLOBERA
CARRETERA MIRAMAR
FUNDACIÓ MIRÓ
TEATRE GREC
MUSEU ARQUEOLÒGIC
MUSEU ETNOLÒGIC
PALAU ALBÉNIZ
PALAU NACIONAL MUSEU D'ART DE CATALUNYA (MNAC)
PALAU VICTÒRIA EUGÈNIA
POBLE ESPANYOL
PALAU ALFONS XIII
PALAU DE CONGRESSOS
FIRA DE BARCELONA
PLAÇA UNIVERS
PALAU CINQUENTENARI
AMPOSTA
MORABOS
AVDA. REINA MA. CRISTINA
PLAÇA ESPANYA
PLAÇA DE BRAUS LES ARENES
PARC JOAN MIRÓ
PARC DE L'ESPANYA INDUSTRIAL
ESTACIÓ BARCELONA SANTS
PLAÇA PAÏSOS CATALANS
PLAÇA DE SANTS
GRAN VIA DE LES CORTS CATALANES
TARRAGONA
LLEIDA
FONT HONRADA
AVINGUDA DEL PARAL·LEL
RONDA LITORAL
MOLL DEL CONTRADIC
MOLL DE LA COSTA
DARSENA DEL MORROT
MOLL SANT BERTRAN
DARSENA SANT BERTRAN
TRANSBORDADOR AERI
MOLL OCCIDENTAL
MOLL BARCELONA
TORRE JAUME I
PORT DE BARCELONA
MOLL NOU
MOLL BALEARS
DARSENA DE LA INDUSTRIA
TORRE SANT SEBASTIÀ
MOLL DELS PESCADORS
MAREMAGNUM
AQUARIUM
IMAX
RAMBLA DE MAR
MOLL D'ESPANYA
MARINA PORT VELL
DARSENA DE COMERÇ
MOLL DE LA BARCELONETA
PASSEIG JOAN DE BORBÓ
MUSEU D'HISTÒRIA DE CATALUNYA
PLATJA DE SANT MIQUEL
PLATJA BARCELONETA
PARC DE LA BARCELONETA
PASSEIG MARÍTIM
HOSPITAL DEL MAR
PLATJA DE LA BARCELONETA
PG. MARÍTIM
HOTEL DE LES ARTS
PLAÇA DELS VOLUNTARIS
VILA OLÍMPICA
MOLL DE MARINA
TORRE MAPFRE
PORT OLÍMPIC
ESCULLERA DE POBLE NOU
MOLL DE XALOC
RONDA SANT PAU
COMTE D'URGELL
RONDA SANT ANTONI
PASSEIG DRASSANES
REIALS DRASSANES MUSEU MARÍTIM
MTO. A COLÓN
RAMBLES
MUSEU DE CERA
PLAÇA REIAL
GRAN TEATRE DEL LICEU
MERCAT BOQUERIA
PALAU DE LA VIRREINA
BIBLIOTECA DE CATALUNYA
CASA DE LA CARITAT
MACBA
UNIVERSITAT
PLAÇA DE LA UNIVERSITAT
RONDA UNIVERSITAT
PLAÇA DE CATALUNYA
PORTAL DE L'ÀNGEL
ESGLÉSIA DEL PI
AJUNTAMENT DE BARCELONA
PALAU DE LA GENERALITAT
PLAÇA S. JAUME
CATEDRAL
AVDA. CATEDRAL
VIA LAIETANA
PALAU DE LA MÚSICA
PLAÇA URQUINAONA
RONDA SANT PERE
SANTA MARIA DEL MAR
MUSEU PICASSO
ANTIC MERCAT DEL BORN
ESTACIÓ DE FRANÇA
PASSEIG DE PICASSO
PASSEIG DE LLUIS COMPANYS
ARC DEL TRIOMF
PALAU DE JUSTÍCIA
PARC DE LA CIUTADELLA
PARC ZOOLÒGIC
PARLAMENT DE CATALUNYA
FONT MONUMENTAL
MNAC
PASSEIG DE PUJADES
ANTIGA ESTACIÓ DEL NORD
AVDA. MERIDIANA
WELLINGTON
LA MARINA
PASSEIG DE CARLES I
PLAÇA DE BRAUS MONUMENTAL
PLAÇA DE TETUAN
PASSEIG DE SANT JOAN
PÇA. MOSSEN JACINT VERDAGUER
AVINGUDA DIAGONAL
SAGRADA FAMÍLIA
PÇA. GAUDÍ
AVINGUDA GAUDÍ
LEPANT
MARINA
LEPANTO
ALCALDE
RAMBLA DE CATALUNYA
PASSEIG DE GRÀCIA
LA PEDRERA
CASA DE LES PUNXES
PLAÇA DOCTOR LETAMENDI
ENRIC GRANADOS
BALMES
VIA AUGUSTA
GRAN DE GRÀCIA
PL. JOAN CARLES I
ARAGÓ
MALLORCA
PROVENÇA
ROSSELLÓ
CÒRSEGA
DIPUTACIÓ
CONSELL DE CENT
VALÈNCIA
MUNTANER
ARIBAU
CASANOVA
VILLARROEL
COMTE BORRELL
VILADOMAT
CALÀBRIA
ROCAFORT
ENTENÇA
VILAMARÍ
LLANÇÀ
AVDA. ROMA
AVDA. MISTRAL
AVINGUDA DE SARRIÀ
JOSEP TARRADELLAS
NUMÀNCIA
NICARAGUA
MARQUÈS DE SENTMENAT
LONDRES
PARÍS
TUSET
TRAVESSERA DE GRÀCIA
PAU CLARÍS
ROGER DE LLÚRIA
BRUC
GIRONA
BAILÈN
ROGER DE FLOR
NÀPOLS
SICÍLIA
SARDENYA
ALÍ BEI
AUSIÀS MARC
CASP
BERLÍN
GUITARD
VALLESPIR
COMTES DE BELL-LLOC
GALILEU
AVINGUDA DE MADRID
REINA MARIA CRISTINA
JOAN GÜELL
MIQUEL ÀNGEL
RECTOR TRIADÓ
BÈJAR
CREU COBERTA
SANT ROC
HOSTAFRANCS